MON AMI MON AMOUR NOW & FOREVER

SHUCHI PATRA

Made with ♥ on the Notion Press Platform
www.notionpress.com

This is my heartfelt gift, dazzling, glistening pearls of my innermost emotions of my intense and passionate love , being overwhelmed , eternally indebted to my best friend, my lover , my former colleague, my life partner, my husband, my raison d' etre

Samiran Patra

This book is also dedicated to the best and most special couple in love, my parents, Dr. Sudha and Prof. R. D. Iyer and all couples who are bound by Eternal Love.

Contents

Contents

Contents

Preface

When two people meet, become , best of friends , fall madly in love, then decide to spend the rest of their lives together, the mystical and magical myriad hues of emotions, the romance, the soul to soul connection, the yearning , the frenzied passions, the melting moments of ecstasy, the working as a team facing all the challenges, the setbacks, the pains, hand in hand traversing the crests and troughs, sailing through good and bad weather, some sweet and sour banters, some hurts and misunderstandings, the going beyond all ego and self-importance, the willingness to sacrifice, the intense wish to see each other happy, to be there for each other through health and sickness. To be always together, as friends, lovers, life partners in life's brief beautiful sojourn!

All these very sublime and intense overflowing emotions are expressed through some poetic pearls of beautiful, nectarine love poems, I have shared in this monument of our Love, I offer my beloved, the love of my life, my life itself, Samiran Patra as my heart, my soul, my core encompassed by his True Love in my book...

Mon Ami

Mon Amour

Now and Forever!

Hope you, the readers relate to the various shades of the canvas of Love, and enjoy your journey through my heart!

Acknowledgements

I express my heartfelt gratitude to my husband Samiran Patra, for undertaking the arduous task of formatting, editing and publishing the book inspite of his busy work schedule.

I also thank esteemed poet and friend Harshad Pandit for sparing his valuable time so gladly for proof reading .

1. You, Me and Our Love's Ocean

You and me, sitting on the white gorgeous sands
Close, cosy, cuddling, gazing at the wondrous waves, our life in silken strands
My soul gazing into your soul's eyes
Precious, priceless togetherness moments, in them our world lies
The vastness of the gigantic ocean
Like love that's just endless, without reason
Stretching miles and miles
Limitless, bringing beatific smiles
Fathomless, so deep
Within the heart, treasures to keep
The hues emerald green, turquoise and blue
Change over the day to a sombre grey anew
As sunset shades, twilight rhythms spread
A tranquillity descends
Dispelling any fears and dread
Like life satiated towards its evening
Prayers and bells ringing
The setting sun shimmering on the dancing waves
Like pulchritude and passion on emotion ridden heart waves

This majestic ocean visible to the eyes, is ephemeral outside,
But it's also within us,
and our soul where beauty resides eternally inside
You, me and our love's ocean
Taking our fill from the amorous elixir, love's nectarine potion!

2. You, I Look In Your yes

I look in your eyes ..such selflessly pure love
Just sweeping me off my feet
Off the face of this earth itself
Off the precariously dangling broken branch
Off the edge of the slippery pointed cliff
Off all the burdens , worries and loads piled up on my heart and yours
Off all pains, sufferings and agonies so infused into our lives
I almost fly on the dreamy clouds with the wings
Of your desires in the azure sky
I love to drown into the very depths of your two pools
Overflowing with such intense passionate love for me
Tis your two wondrous sparks
Lighting up my dark corners
I see in your eyes my darling
A person, a great human being, of class, calibre, par excellence
A heart of gold, so pure, so magical., such feeling, emotion
such sensitivity, compassion..such fathomless depth
My lover, my life partner, my true faithful friend
My saviour, raison d'etre
My strength, My very Life!

3. The Pink Pulchritudinous Panorama!

Pink Pulchritude, as we fly
aboard the amorous night sky
Such beautiful hues of pink, amber,
nature's stunningly gorgeous face
A passionate embrace
Dream or reality?
Sliding gently into fantasy
Ready to drown into its fathomless oceans
A mellifluous melody
Enraptures, enthrals, spellbinding
Are we two or one?
Far from the madding crowds
Far from the madding worries and thunderous
painful dark clouds
Amidst heavenly nature's paradise
Silence, serene tranquillity, divine guise
Solitude, sweet and pristine
Togetherness!

4. You're the only one

You're the only one who is mine
In every sense, every perspective
The only one in whose heart, only I reside eternally
And who totally pervades my being
Drenching my core with your Selfless, boundless ocean of love
Why did fate conspire to take away our joys
To fade our many splendored love,
Our world was oozing elixir, of pure, nectarine love
Beyond all boundaries, all realms
Passionate and insane, it gushed ahead
A river fiercely forging ahead overcoming huge boulders of obstacles and challenges
Prickly stones of pains and woes
But fate was successful in destroying our carefree abandon
The peace and security, of blessedness,
Of an inner faith, strength, courage
The feeling that 'All is Well' that just seeped through every pore
Infusing pulchritude, passion, zeal, enthusiasm
In every moment
Even over the years now, in pulsating pain spasms
In searing streaks of setbacks
In lightning bolts of traumas,

You're the only one who makes me feel complete
Who never lets me feel let down
As its only me, who dwells in your heart
You're the only one who gives much more than you get
You're the confluence of my passion and emotions
That merge into your own
In body, heart and soul
Ever eternally,
You're the only one who is mine!

5. What's falling in love

Falling in love! True love can only happen once
That's the love that's destined in heavens above
The love that has equal fire on both sides
Attracted to each other like powerful magnets
Like the waves crashing on the ocean
Like the rain clouds coming thundering to embrace the earth and
Drenching it to the core
Or like the tumultuous and rapturous river
That forges through mountains and valleys
To meet and merge into the ocean
Falling in love experience is out of the world, ethereal, cosmic, celestial
It's mesmerizing, catapulting you to a different world altogether
It gives you limitless blissful happiness,
you are spellbound, as though bewitched, under its enchanting spell
You are not you at all, nor are you present in the time,
in the worldly realm
Your world is different, far away from the real world around you
You are on cloud 9, flying high on dreamy clouds of fantasy and fascination

You are like a fish, always dying, pining to be in the water again
Day and night are the same
With only one dream in your forever wakeful eyes, of being with your lover
Every moment of separation is a torment
But the moments give a thrill and a passionate longing to be together
There is a sweet pain, that's ineffable
The looking forward to the encounter itself infuses the heart with an overflowing hope and joy
There is an intoxication and delirious feverish fervour
The moments of secret rendezvous, escape from all around you
Thrilling, exciting, electrifying and exhilarating!
That's falling in love
And it truly, happens Only Once!

6. Love beyond Science

A powerful magnetic force
Or was it a force beyond any science
A force straight from the gates of heaven
That pulled me towards you
From two lands afar
From two languages and cultures so poles apart

When I fell in love with you
The spark was ignited and fuelled with every passing moment
Defying every scientific reason
Submitting to a pull above all gravity
We were literally magically drifting in a new beautiful space realm
You became my moon, and I your moonlight
Our love vibes, our intense feelings became twinkling stars
Our paradisiacal world, the fantastic galaxy

Much more spellbinding than any spell of science
Much more mesmerizingly attractive than any laws of attraction
Our reactions to each other's feelings, love darts
Beyond all Newton's laws

Our chemistry, so electrifying
Our bond, is there such strength in any existing chemical or physical bond yet?
Our love story more thrilling than any sci-fi novel or action thriller ever made
Our friendship, our soul connection, is divine, preordained and eternal!

7. Beyond all words

I know, you, your love
Your emotions, your actions
Are beyond all words
No words can measure up to them
No words can do justice in describing them
Though words often pour out
From my overwhelmed, gratified heart
Often they shine and sparkle
Like fresh morning dewdrops
In joyous mirth
Or dazzle like brilliant and twinkling stars
Feeling pulchritudinous, alluring, basking in your adoration
Or surge out gushing unobstructed spontaneous
Like a river just impatient for her union with the mighty ocean
And yes they do bleed ink
As my heart bleeds for you
I write my soul, my truthful emotions, my heart out
No poetic illusion or fantasy, dreams or hyperboles
Just to embellish my verse
No I need none of it
As you, your love my dearest beloved,
Is beyond all words!

8. Never ever leave me alone

Never ever leave me alone,
Without you, not even my shadow is my own
Nothing in the vast universe is worthwhile
No delicacies, no palatial house, no vacation, no luxury, no style
Without you, I'm a fish out of water, gasping for breath..
I'm a body without a soul,
I'm a barren land, no greens
Without you, I'm a sky
Cloudless, starless
Breezeless, still
No sun, no moon, no planets
Without you
I can't face any single moment
Every fraction of time, an excruciating torment
A part of you, inseparable
Never ever leave me alone!

9. I dream of you

I dream, my every dream should be about you, only you
That nature, the whole universe will conspire to make it real too
I dream, to be with you in eternal trance
Your hand in mine, swaying in carefree abandon in a delightful dance
Let's don wings of fantasy
Our hearts and souls entwined in divine ecstasy
I dream, of you, resplendent in breath-taking aura and radiant glow
Your heart ablaze with zeal, enthusiasm and passion flow
From the core of my heart, is an intense burning wish
To rewind my life, to go back in time, being in love with you, insane, feverish
As free birds we fly high riding the thundering mischievous cloud
No cares, no woes, no worries, singing aloud
Dreaming about you
My entire life flowing, in this blissful river of your dream,
Reliving each moment anew
Life is a sleep, and love is its dream
And you have lived, if you have loved!

10. Till my last breath

Till my last breath dearest,
I want you to be there for me
I want to feel you,
Feel your breath, listen to your heartbeats
Feel them merge with mine
Feel your secure arms around me,
Our bodies, hearts and souls entwined,
As I snuggle close to you!

Till my last breath my true, closest friend
I want to feel your overflowing, overpowering love
I want to be the river forever surging to be one with her vast mighty ocean
I want to be your friend, soulmate, confidante
Your princess, your honour, my esteemed prince charming
Forever, eternally young and beautiful, only for you!

Till my last breath my beloved love
I want to give my all to you
I want to drench you with the heaviest showers
Passionate rain clouds bursting upon you
My bewitching gaze, my amour, my pulchritude, my playfulness,

my nectarine love
To feel the thrill of being in love, everyday
I want you to feel most special, most wanted always
Till my last breath my saviour,
I want to care, protect and serve you
In every weather, health or sickness
Shielding and supporting you through our storms
Praying for you, may God give you my life, if need arises
Want to see you strong and smiling, full of zeal and vigour
To Feel secure, at peace and tranquil in your clasp
As the bells ring, my world slowly disappears
The last breath I take happily,
safe in your embrace
getting ready, heeding His call, for God's heavenly grace!

11. When I belong to You

When I belong to you
I'm right within you,
As you are within me
My feelings are not mine,
As they are entwined with yours
My heartbeats can feel yours,
As yours feel mine
They beat in tandem
To the rhythm and tune of our love
When I belong to you,
All my desires, my joys
My struggles, my pains
Are yours too
And yours, mine
Your being upset, angry, sad ever
Bleeds me like innumerable swords piercing my fabric,
storming into my mind, tumultuously
burning into my heart and soul
I may like, love people , care , be fond of
I may be tempted for adventures
But can it ever be without you?
In my thoughts, in my senses

In my innermost feelings, emotions
You are the one, who's a permanent resident
You are the one, inseparable,
As the moon from moonlight
As the stars from the night
As the greens from nature,
As the waves from the ocean
As heartbeats from the heart,
And the breath from life,
As the soul from the body
I am not just me,
When I belong to YOU!

When I belong to you
I'm right within you,
As you are within me
My feelings are not mine,
As they are entwined with yours
My heartbeats can feel yours,
As yours feel mine!

12. Gifts from You, my Love

I don't need any greeting cards or videos,
I don't need expensive jewellery,
I don't need stylish , valuable cosmetics
Nor any ravishing gorgeous clothes
Nor cute, adorable cuddly soft toys
I don't need our pics on pillows or t-shirts or mugs
Or dazzling on crystals
Nor any expensive musical instruments or music systems
Nor any extravagant lunches or dinners
Nor any pricy vacations
I don't need grand, posh palatial accommodation or refurbishing or
Renovation, beautification of our houses
I need you healthy and strong as can be
That's the most invaluable wealth I will ever have!
I need you forever in my heart to fill it with your adorable love and its bliss
I need you to only keep me in your heart,
To infuse it with my passion and intense overflowing emotions
I need freshness and thrill in our romance

I need you forever in my home
Built with your abundant shower,
Of warmth, care, affection, faithfulness and loyalty
Utter understanding, friendship beyond measure
My priceless treasure
I want to cherish our beautiful memories,
And revisit those very special, precious pages of our life,
With you, and make many more amazing memories
To never have any secrets from each other
To share everything, every day
To be just inseparable
Our bond so sweet, unique, unbreakable!
To feel you, every moment of each day

To forever drown in your
Selfless, boundless ocean of love,
I want us to reside in each other's hearts,
Our souls to be ONE,
Eternally!

13. Come back my friend, I miss you so much

I miss you my friend, come back
That soul which first attracted mine
I miss that friend who came close to my heart
Spontaneously, unknowingly
Unplanned, unhindered
Like waves that crash to the shore
That person who felt me even from far
Without touching me, touched my heart and soul
That heart which bled for my pains
Which wanted to kiss away my tears
Fill my world with only smiles and laughter
That mind which reasoned but always obeyed its heart
The heart that became mine even before the mind and intellect knew
I miss that surge of intense overflowing strong emotions
That felt my heart, that rode
On its tumultuous waves
That wanted to sooth the agonising and piercing wounds
That wanted to be the strong secure pillar
To my fearful and terrified mind

I miss 'that' you my friend
Take me close so close that my breath merges with yours
And I don't feel my pain anymore
As it's fully encompassed with your warmth, cosy comfort and secure understanding clasp of love
Take me close
Don't let any distance sting and bite
It's so unbearable
Our nectarine love
You were and are my pride, my strength and my satisfaction
You are my raison d'etre
Then where are you lost?
Why are you so lost?
Your pain your struggles numbed you so much?
My life is a boat that's about to capsize
It's losing balance
The rudder is getting broken
My eyes, empty and overflowing with sadness
Looking for blessings and protection from the creator
Feeling a fear a dread
Feeling lost to the world ..Meaningless
But a candle of hope flickering dimly
Before it extinguishes and the light goes out
Before darkness of despair sets in
Come back my friend, I miss and yearn for you!

14. The Dazzling Brightest Star on my life's horizon

This twinkling and dazzling, the Brightest star
On my horizon, brightens it, bringing warmth and good cheer
This soothing cool zephyr
His smile so infectious
His eyes full of feeling and good intent
His demeanour friendly and helpful
His admirable maturity laced with a childlike innocence
The child in him, still alive
Persona mesmerizing
That's his Charisma!

Adding to the charm,
A class intellect, a knowledge powerhouse
Tall, dark and handsome, my knight in shining armour
Smart, dashing and resourceful
Nothing's impossible for him
Ladies are charmed, men are impressed, inspired
Kids in awe, elders drawn by the warmth and utter respect

His words, his knack for convincing
That's his Charisma!
A fragrant flower in life's garden,
A guiding light in darkness
His giving up of Ego and Arrogance
His friendly and down to earth attitude
And going out of the way to help those in need
Not just makes his office team his fans
But bowls over his adversaries
That's his Charisma!
His grit and determination,
His sacrificing selfless soul burning like a candle,
for all he dearly loves
His courage and commitment
Everything about him, makes me fall in love with him,
all over again, day after day
That's his Charisma,
The Dazzling Brightest Star on my life's horizon!

15. Truly One

Every moment with you
I've lived a lifetime
You are the cool zephyr blowing
Pervading my being, every moment,
Making my heart beat and sing like a musical wind chime
You are my poetry in motion, giving every verse its rhythm and rhyme
Unthinkable, unimaginable, impossible,
Are moments without you
Your ambrosial touch has aromatized every bit of my physical being and inner core too
Through your pure, selfless, unconditional ,overflowing love
Your heart has encompassed mine, your soul and mine are one
Where is the distance
We are truly one, in every moment, every instance!

16. The table is laid

The table is laid
For you and me
Chosen in heaven
To meet and love
Like never before or ever after
The sea of our life spread out before us
The incessant waves of our dreams and desires
Of ups and downs
Of little joys and big struggles
On the colourful horizon of our world together
Let's drink up to the wine of joy and mirth
Let's eat a toast of wisdom
Lets have a meal together of understanding, care, and compassion
And a desert to top it all of the sweet nothings, the nectar of oneness
Let's sing and dance as long as we can
Banishing all the black clouds of anguish and pain
Sharing the oceans of fantasy
Let's revel in the beauty of our bond
and pray to the heavens above
To give us peace , content and love not for a lifetime

But till eternity
We are part of each other, not today or tomorrow
But forever and ever
Come...the table is laid
For you and me!

17. What is True Love

True Love does not happen because you decide it, or your heart demands it
Or you have attraction, infatuation or crush on someone
Or because you are in the idea, Dream World of this falling in love
Or because you get obsessed with the idea and it happens at the drop of a hat
Or everytime you see or meet someone beautiful or attractive or impressive
True Love happens because it is destined to, and the heavens have ordained
True Love happens when hearts connect, wavelengths match
True Love happens when someone wants to delve deep into your heart
Wants to listen to your innermost feelings, understand them
True love is so deserving,
it proves by action, not just by words and has courage of conviction
It Honours commitment and can sacrifice its all, but never imposes, is forgiving
it can never hurt, insult, demean...never corrupted and impure and has no deception or fakeness

What is true love ?

It's that Love which is life itself, pure bliss

It has immense mutual respect, adoration and passion

It has care and understanding, and cannot see its love hurt in pain, sadness

It always strives for its love's happiness

True Love is total surrender, losing heart mind, body and soul to love

True Love connects first with the heart and soul and then has physical longings or both happen simultaneously

It's a direct connection, a feeling of oneness

It's the feeling of two bodies, one soul, of being ONE, inseparable

True Love is divinity, transcending every realm,

True Love is beyond births and deaths, undaunting, enduring, ethereal and eternal!

18. Let's go back in time

Let's go back in time
Just You and Me
Come again, like a bright enchanting rainbow,
In my life even then clouded with dark clouds
Come again, a cool, comforting caress of the merry zephyr,
Soothing my scorching mind and heart
Bringing a new zeal, joy and good cheer
Let me be a raging, tumultuous wave,
Crashing down upon your hearts shore
Drenching you with my passionate, intense and overflowing love

Let's go back in time
To those fulfilled magical moments
Not a care or worry in the world,
As carefree as birds soaring high above all mundane trifles
Just absorbing the thrill of the heart throbbing rendezvous
The insane and reckless lovers let loose
An incessantly, unstoppable, unquenchable thirst
To meet, to come together
To touch each other's souls,
To dive into each other's hearts
Drowning Deep inside, the fathomless depths

Crossing layers untouched, unexplored, unknown
Sharing our lives and our innermost thoughts,
Feelings and emotions
Feeling and enjoying the unbelievable magical vibes
Inching closer and closer
Revelations and discoveries
Just revelling in the sweet nectarine togetherness
Let's go back in time,
Just You and Me!

19. When you fall in love with your best friend

When you are friends
Coming closer by the day, then by the moments
As a friend, you would feel for your friend
In joys, happy and in sorrow, sad too
But still you would return to your own world
Your fate, destiny would be different
When you fall in love with your friend
Your worlds converge into one
Your friend is your world now, so everything affects you as much
it does the friend
Your destinies get linked
As friends, you could remain apart, but in touch
As friends in love, you are inseparable
Both in heart and soul
Bonded forever
As well as physically pulled closer and closer
Two magnets that can never stay apart
That every separation
Creates a longing
To be together again, always!

Every moment you are together,
In spirit and in heart
So much so that you can feel each other,
Wherever you go
Holding on to each other
In life's every weather
However winding, thorny and pebbly the road
Being a constant, never flinching, Unwavering companion
A rock solid support
In storms, floods and endless rain
Of troubles, struggles, calamities and pain
Whenever, Wherever
You're meant to be together!
You carry one another inside you
In your heart
Part of your soul,
As you become One!

20. Now and Forever

Now and forever I'll be yours,
All my world is you, yours
My desires, my dreams are yours
All my prayers and hopes are yours !
Now and forever
You are only mine!
Your world encompasses me
Your fiercest passions possess me,
Your overflowing love, drowns me in its fathomless depths
Now and forever
We are tied by the strongest threads of our hearts
Our souls have become friends since long
As we drink from the nectarine elixir
Quenching our thirst,
Again with more thirst for each other, unquenchable
Now and Forever!

21. Your soul kissed mine

Oh! That feeling, that touch!
Your soul touched, kissed mine
Even before your first touch, first kiss
You made me feel yours
When our hearts and souls became friends
Much before we did
Did they recognize each other ?
Even amidst so much disparity,
Such a vast distance between
Our lands, our languages and cultures
But this distance disappeared
when we met, coming closer each day!
It was as though finally we came home
Were we searching for each other,
All our life, lives before too?
And the search finally ended with our coming together,
Destined, preordained!
Our union first of hearts and souls
Before our physical union!
We were in the same city, even quite close by
Though strangers,
Little did we know we were to meet,

Drown in insane love,
Our rendezvous with love, to last a lifetime
Adventure, thrill, magic and a dream fulfilled
Our friendship, our courtship, our marriage
Still reminiscent of those magical moments
Oh that feeling, that touch
Your soul touched, kissed mine
Even before your first touch, first kiss!

22. It's only you

Who peeped and searched inside me
Who loved the delicate, sensitive inner core
Who revelled in the richness of my soul
Who became intoxicated with the fragrance In the garden of my emotions

It's only you
Who tried to fathom the depths of my heart
Who had intense urge to explore the vastness
Of my mind and heart
Who never ever let me down

It's only you
Who cherished me in happy and sad times
With all my pains, tries to make me smile
Who still makes me feel beautiful,
Inspite of the ephemeral, evanescent youth

It's only you
Who's my steadfast support
My strongest pillar of strength
Who feels my heartaches

Connects to my soul
It's only you
Who's still my friend since ages
who stuck on through thick and thin
Who was and is a soothing balm
on the scars of my wounded heart
It's only you
Who truly cares, shares everything
Who makes me feel important, so special... from my innermost core , depths of my soul
I cherish this You, forever, my love, my life!

23. The Fragrance of Rajnigandha (tuberose)

'Rajnigandha' or tuberose
my favourite flower
Its captivating perfumed fragrance
Just as my beloved
spreading the fragrance of his love in my life
And in my love struck yearning heart
The simple and white beauty of Rajnigandha
Is like his spell,
Full of simplicity and purity,
bringing peace and serenity in our life
Every moment brings only his dreams in my eyes
I can feel his presence in every heart beat
I wish I could just draw out all his pain his troubles
his obstacles
Just like the honey bee sucking on the flower
And drown him into the nectar of my love
To plunge deeper and deeper
Into the captivating depths of infinite blissful
tender passion
O Rajnigandha, your aroma intoxicating

Enticing and mesmerizing
Brings thrill, life and adventure into our lives
and fills my heart with his fragrant love
To remain fresh, pure and simple, like
The fragrance of Rajnigandha!

24. For you I will always be beautiful

You never looked at me,
Always looked within me
You never saw the book by the cover
You delved into its contents
You peeped inside my heart and soul
Even being bereft of external beauty,
You saw , felt, absorbed the inner beauty
You made me feel so magically beautiful !
Under the mesmerizing spell of your love,
from a duck, a swan I became
Your true love awakened in me a sense
Of such pulchritude, passion,
An alluring, attractive , aura, a charm
Bringing about a radiance, a dazzling disarming demeanour
Beauty is not skin deep
And that you proved beyond doubt
With a love that will always see me beautiful
Even as age rapidly takes over
When the charm , gleam and sheen of youth wean
When health takes a toll on the physical self

Like trees once with luscious green foliage,
Now same but rough, withered, wrinkled
For you, I will always be beautiful,
Not just for your eyes that can see the outside
But the eyes of your soul that has already become
One with mine!

25. Drowning in Love

Just as I think I've hit the rock bottom of
The sea bed
I keep rapidly getting thrust deeper and deeper
Drowning recklessly
Into the fathomless depths,
Of the boundless ocean
Of Your Love
Limitless, profound, selfless, enduring
Classy, passionate, ethereal ,
Divine!

26. Then and Now

It was You and Me then
It's We now
Those Golden Moments
So bright, luminous
Shining with sunny radiance
Youth and True Love
In all its seraphic splendour
Exuberance, enthusiasm, effervescence
Roses, lilies and dancing daffodils
Precious priceless gifts, are the Memories
Part of me, part of you
Heavenly bliss to drown into them
To revisit, relive each moment, so special
To forget myself, totally get lost in them
Then and Now
Light and Darkness
Stars dazzling once, wowing the horizon
Now on the ground, pale,
Lost their Lustre their twinkle
But Stars nonetheless
Now it's Us
In every weather,

Tears and smiles together
Infused, dripping in Love
Battling shoulder to shoulder,
Praying to Him above
Our Souls the same,
Fused into each other
Appearances changed
Like chiselled diamonds
Awe-inspiring, phenomenal
Then and Now!

27. Miss You So Much

Miss you so much
Every moment, impatient, incomplete as such
Separation torments
Lacklustre, decrepit moments
But we are warriors
Each other's saviours
Together, loving, caring and fighting our battles, as a TEAM
However the problems, pains, tensions as powerful as they seem
We have come so far though it seems only yesterday we met
This feeling need to preserve and cherish I bet
We are One, Inseparable
In minds, hearts and souls, invincible!

28. You, in Me

You are ingrained in me
Like the thoughts in the mind,
Like the swelling emotions
That are waves crashing upon the heart's shores

You are imprinted on my soul
Like memories
Like hurts and pains
Like the beauty and bliss of childhood

You are the colours
That have splashed upon me, making me feel beautiful
that have coloured my heart, that have painted my soul in vibrant, radiant hues

You have set a benchmark
I try to see you in everyone that draws closer
My heart expects the same words, actions, gestures
That made me fall in love with you
You are the medicine
the only medicine for my agonising pains
that heals and embalms

that tries to replace every scar
With the sign of your love

You are my addiction,
you and only you I forever crave
Not a breath to take without you
Not a moment to endure in separation!

29. Monuments of our Love

Neither flashy nor extravagant
Nor structures of architectural grandeur
The very simple things, places we visited when in love
Became monuments of our love!
The snacks vendor at the lane entrance,
The coffee house near by
The training centre where we met and
Where our love was born,
And blossomed
The roads where our bike sped in abandon
The garden we used to visit and overstay till it got dark
Convincing the caretaker we were not up to any mischief,
The restaurant we secretly dined
The apartment where my beloved stayed
Going there escaping
From our offices and training
The thrill and heart pounding,
Excitement
The secret rendezvous
The bench on the hilltop

Lovers gazing at the moon
On a full moon night
Then drowning in each other's eyes
Lost in an ethereal world
A witness, these monuments of our love!

30. Tale of a Rose and a card

What was this Rose and card tale
On remembrance, often a smile or laugh to bring does it fail
We had just become friends
And slowly coming closer becoming more than friends
Practice after class was over
We were the only two in the room with the server
We practiced, got talking
When I wished all my troubles could end
As a patient understanding ear he did lend
Sensing my pain, overcome
By an intense desire to make me feel loved ,
A hug and a failed kiss
My utter shock made it miss
As we were still only friends
And though we did not fight
I just explained, I was grateful for his moral support
Other things at this moment not right
On reaching home, in our usual call,
Made my hurt clear, the line had been crossed
The next day as my auto sped, towards my office,

I saw him waiting on the roadside
His hands concealing something behind
He requested if he could accompany me in the auto
I somehow could not refuse
He sat and looking into my eyes, full of love, and an apology
immediately handed me a rose and a card
That said
I am sorry I hurt you, please give me another chance,
I don't want to lose your friendship,
It's very precious to me
It was so unexpected, such a sweet lovely surprise
A romantic way to say sorry
Totally making up for what had happened
My hurt by now had disappeared!
Our journey continued happily and still does
Entwined in the fragrance of so many roses
Fighting against many a thorn
But the story of a Rose and a card is still, and
Will always be special!

31. Lost Lover

Where are you, my love?
Among the multifarious roles you play dear,
I search for my lover
My lost lover
Or my hidden lover who does surface occasionally
Lost in multitude of pains and woes
Lost in a huge mountain of responsibilities and duties
Of changed situations and priorities
Lost in a dark dense forest of wild worries and complexities
Among the myriad hues of your persona
I long to see the beautiful dashing,
Multi-coloured hue of my lover
I long for the same passionate fervour
The same restlessness and yearning for me
The same delighting me with lovely surprises
Just to see me smile
His eyes overflowing with nectarine love
Full of purity, selflessness and satisfaction
Who would go to lengths just to meet me
Who would be so inseparable
Who would not sleep without talking for hours,

late into the night
Whose heart would bleed for my pains,
Who would wipe away and wish away every tear from my eye
Among so many facets of your personality
I miss my old crazy impatient and reckless lover
Going out of the way, breaking rules,
Just chilling in wild carefree abandon
Secretly rushing to many a thrilling rendezvous
A friend, a soulmate, a lover, a colleague, a husband
I know they are all important shades of your canvas
But my favourite, the one I miss from the depths of the core
I know, can feel him in there
Now in another unique flavour
In so many actions and decisions
In so many sacrifices
In so much understanding and feeling
In beautiful gestures, surprises and love splashing through them
Yet
I just want that friend back who fell insanely in love with me!

32. Melting Moments of Ecstasy

Let me dive deep into your eyes
Let me blissfully drown, without efforts
As the gigantic waves of emotions and passion, intimate desires in your heart,
Crash upon the shores of mine
Let me ride high above them
Dancing on the tumultuous waves
To your soul's mellifluous melody
In these melting moments
Let me lose myself..Beyond all consciousness
The mind and its turmoil, quietened,
As our souls in unison, watch our bodies unite
Our love's fiery passion fire ignite
Illuminate every nook and corner
Sweetened by the overflowing nectar
Lips sealed in ambrosial lock,Lead the way, into a paradisiacal world
As every fragment in divine ecstasy
Merges with yours, Losing every separateness
Becoming integrally One!

33. My Valentine in Quarantine

Oh My Love,
my valentine, In Quarantine
I can hear you, feel you
You are so close
And yet the walls separate us
These walls of our destiny
Want to divide us keep us apart
My longings My yearnings rise
Like a bird I want to fly to you
Breaking the cages we are imprisoned
Prisoners of fate..Disease and pain
However like tsunamis huge and gigantic
Our waves of emotions and passion
Will ride above them and crash
On the shores of our hearts
I can feel and hear your breath
As my breath merges with yours
I can hear and feel your heartbeats
As they rhyme with mine

The lover in me today becomes the air
The breeze, the wind
That gently flows into you
Soothing!, caressing every bit
Of your body, heart and soul
Tender and sublime, they touch you
Becoming One with you
With ever eternal elixir enchanting
Oozing overflowing nectar
So fulfilling so satiating
Every thirst quenched
Come my dear, let's celebrate
Though virtually, in spirit
Let's dance and sing
To the melody and rhythm,
of the magical, everlasting, fantasy filled fountain of love
My Valentine, in Quarantine!

34. You are my magnificent Moon

The sky on a full moon night
Stars dazzling, the heart joyous, so bright
The divine aura, the celestial shower
Of the majestic magnificent moon
One in the azure, dreamy ceiling above
And one, my friend, my beloved, here on earth, beside me
My love, You, are my magnificent Moon!

35. A confession from the core

I met you, my heart thirsty for true love
I was in a maddening maze, mind in a horrific haze
Even then, enveloped by problems and pains, looking for showers of loving rains
You looked inside my heart, loaded and heavy
With burdens and worries
You wanted to shower me with all your attention and affection
You wanted to drown me in your overwhelming magnetic love
You wanted to wipe my tears .and bring smiles
Fill my agonised heart with pulchritude and passion
You entered my meandering maze with courage
A soldier full of craze
My devilish destiny, wounded you too
Yet all these years, my armour, my sword were you
As I fought all calamities and faced all struggles
My love, you understood my feelings, my desires, my wishes
You respected them and gave them a place above yours
Even if that meant sacrificing your own
I salute your love, there wasn't ever or can never ever be another even close

Now as the black darkness envelopes
My sky touching problems and pains more severe, grown manifold
You, still my steadfast sail,
My only hope, as the boat rocks dangerously
Your embrace comforting, soothing, strengthening, as you take all my troubles in your fold
I feel guilty at times
Your life would have been full of radiance and bliss
Your dreams and desires all fulfilled
Your journey without any obstacles and joyous
This load will be within me till my last breath
O my love, if I could but give my life
Just to see you as radiant and lustrous as before
As carefree and full of joyous mirth as before
As full of luxurious health and strength as before
To see your life full of ecstatic bliss,
A paradise!

36. The Love in my Life

The love in my life
Saves me from drowning in the depths of despair
It's a lighthouse that guides the ship of my life through choppy seas
It's a soothing balm on the wounds of my heart
It's a healing light when the heart is in torment, bleeding
It makes me smile even amidst tears
It is the ambrosial nectar that sweetens all bitter moments of life
It's the many lamps that light up every dark corner in me
The Love in my life
The Blessing, the Gift priceless
Holding on to me, with Faith and Dedication
Embedded so deep, in the fathomless heart, into the very Core!

37. Only YOU and ME

It's only you and me
In this fathomless life's sea
Dancing, crashing with destiny's giant waves
Our nectarine innocent love, peaceful abandon it craves
None can ever with loving trust
Stay long in our heart's crust
They warm, touch and then end up in indifference, callous hurt
It's only YOU and ME
Forever entwined, fused into
One, yet so free!

38. The night came to an end, but the play would not

Under the tangerine ceiling, on a serene, tranquil night
As we sit by the crashing waves, the play of life,
our life enfolds

As we flip our memory book page by page
Looking into the deep pools of overflowing emotions
Our first meeting by chance, our friendship, falling in love

Our battle to fulfil our promises and commitments
The play it's acts as directed by destiny
Our struggles, our setbacks, our joys, our pains
We faced together, courage and faith, a team
As we revisited our play, through beautiful memories
Bringing some special moments to life
We laughed, we cried, we just let our hearts take over and before
we could realise
The night came to an end
But the play would not!

39. Perpetually in Love

I'm perpetually in love
Every moment as soft as a dove
The blissful feeling, the ecstasy
Is it real or fantasy
The day in hectic activity, with the inner beauty of love blossoms
Never a moment away, the heart and soul, always near, the twosome
The night dressed up as a new bride
Bringing all the days tensions, pains in its stride
The ecstatic moments of the night
Fill the heart with zeal, to tide over the next day making it bright
Reliving rich moments from the past
How the movie flashes fast
We, are we not what we were?
Let's forget every struggle, pain, heartache ever
I want to lose myself totally in you, to live,
All my happiness, my moments to give..
you are my raison d'etre, my saviour my only true friend
I'm in perpetual love, my dear, till the very end!

40. Lavender Blossoms

Oh blooming bewitchingly beautiful blessed lavender blossoms
Take me into your fold
Wrap me in your fragrant and soft soothing embrace
As I lie in your loving embrace adorned by your alluring caressing petals
My darling, my love, my life, come
Let us go back in time once more
When we were forever drowned in the ecstatic world of dreams, sweet romantic love
Our hearts, souls and our passions on fire
Without a care, without a worry
no responsibility, no fearful thoughts
Just blissfully absorbing the mad love vibes
Completely enjoying the secret rocking ravishing rendezvous
Endless eternal to be one with each other this life and beyond
And with the lavender blossoms!

41. Looking into your eyes

Looking into your eyes
Let me drown deep into those azure pools
I see my love, my world, my entire life there
I see our dreams, our joys, our sweet moments,
I see our battles, our struggles we fight together
I see you are my rising sun, the light and brilliance, the illumination of my life
Looking into your eyes, I see my raison d'etre
My paradise, my heart, my soul!

42. The blazing reunion

The fiery sun, Tangerine,
Turns into Crimson, Carmine,
All passions and fires alight.
The reunion at long last after so many struggles and fight
The heart, soul and bodies impatient,
Merging, dissolving, drowning into each other every moment
Just as the night sky aglow with the sun's magical myriad hues
Every breath, into breath, every heartbeat into heartbeat does fuse
We are both only, One
With heavens blessings just begun!

43. It's only you

It's only you
Who peeped and searched inside me
Who loved the delicate, sensitive inner core
Who revelled in the richness of my soul
Who became intoxicated with the fragrance in
the garden of my emotions

It's only you
Who tried to fathom the depths of my heart
Who had intense urge to explore the vastness
of my mind and heart
Who never ever let me down

It's only you
Who cherished me in happy and sad times
With all my pains, tries to make me smile
Who still makes me feel beautiful,
Inspite of the ephemeral, evanescent youth
It's only you
Who's my steadfast support
My strongest pillar of strength
Who feels my heartaches

Connects to my soul
It's only you
Who's still my friend since ages
who stuck on through thick and thin
Who was and is a soothing balm
on the scars of my wounded heart
It's only you
Who truly cares, shares everything
Who makes me feel important, so special from my innermost core, depths of my soul
I cherish this You, forever, my love, my life!

44. Hold on to the night

Oh can I hold on to this night
Never to take flight
Clutching every delicate moment
The heartaches, pains, tensions giving vent
The azure skies in gay abandon roar,
The soft fluffy dancing clouds, to high heavens soar

The stars shyly peep
Over our passions so deep
The raindrops sounding like anklets,
The overflowing desires, the feverish fervour,
small quivering, trembling rivulets
Bubbling to be one with the mighty sea
Embrace me, heal me, see

Behold, the night of delight
As we are bathed with heavenly light
Fare you well, to go on call of duty, my brave knight in shining armour,
My restless breaths without you will clamour
To see you, feel you, how will my heart endure
The separation, the moments will be painful sure

I'll hold on to every coming night
In sweet remembrance of tonight
The celestial benevolent moon, my messenger
As you and me look at him, together
We'll revel and lose ourselves in the moment
Won't be very long, but baby I'll be missing you every moment
Then we'll meet in our dreams
In silvery, starry moonlight streams
As the night swiftly fleeting
With sweet intoxication till the next meeting
Sing and gaily dance, holding on to the night
Before arrives the new dawn bright!

45. I'll be Missing you, till we meet again

The lump in my throat
Tears stream, just unstoppable
God wants us to be away,
Why the frequent separation
Stinging heartache with worry and tension

On the call of duty, fighting against all odds
He's our soldier brave, courageous
My heart aches for the tribulations
he faces even though with a smile
My heart he's taken away with him

Miles across, near, far wherever we are
I believe that my heart is safe, inside his
Beating together
Yet I'll be missing you, love
More with the spaces between us and above

Distance makes the heart grow fonder they say
But it aches all the way

The melancholy mind meanders
When will this stop it wonders
Let it suffer a little more

Or is this to make us yearn and pine
How do I console this delicate heart of mine ?
Every night in my dreams, I'll see, feel you
Won't be long, wish time just flew
I'll be Missing you always, till we meet again!

46. Into the fathomless ocean

My dearest, my love, my life
Whenever the dark black clouds threaten, hover
You are my protective cover
You are the soothing zephyr
My pains, my heartaches you decipher
You are the serendipitous cloud
That showers me with joy and my heart shouts aloud
Your love is overwhelming, encompassing,
Into every bit of my heart and soul, penetrating
I'm the bubbling gushing river surging into you
the cool fathomless ocean
At his mere touch, she trembles, quivers with passion
Merging into his wholeness, becoming complete
She is blessed by the infinite!

47. You are only mine

My love, you are tough and your mind is strong
Yet gentle and tender as a cool, calming, loving breeze
To convey your feelings and emotions, in times good and bad
You hold my hand and your eyes say it all
While I pour my gratitude for your deep fathomless love and understanding
I want to cherish and hold on to all the precious moments
When you overwhelm me with your commitment and courage and selflessness
Your affection and love overflowing, I can see it in your eyes
Now all that we have, our bond is so strong
Is pain, struggles and sufferings stronger than our love?
From this life to beyond, our connection is soul to soul
All I have, my treasure in life is you,
You have stolen my heart long back and the sweet rhythm of your love I can feel as it beats
There is no one but me in your heart
Only you are the permanent resident of my heart forever and ever
Without any thoughts of guilt
For any mistakes or hurts that have happened between us
You are and will always be only mine!

48. My Streethawk

The series I used to really enjoy
My heart beat faster, and I used to love the thrill
The spine chilling action
I waited every week, for this handsome, brave and courageous superhero who would curb crime and punish the guilty
Was always on an exciting mission
Then entered my real life superhero
His bike as it stopped in front of my gate
To lift me off into the thrilling, dreamy realms
And my heart skipped many beats
The helmet hiding his face, he took off
The same style the same mannerism
Oh how I loved to wait for my streethawk
My life hero who was destined to be my love, my life
My everything
On a mission 'Love'
Still remember vividly and smile
My streethawk!

49. Oceans of Fantasy

Come give your hand in mine
As the Tangerine sky turns to Carmine
Come let's drown into the pink pulchritude of the night sky
Or should we together with wondrous wings of desire, fly?
Come, share with me the oceans of fantasy
The frenzied waves of our passions into eternal ecstasy
Let's surround ourselves with angel like rhythm
Sing and dance to the tunes of phantasm
Let's dive into each other's fascinating pools of azure
Getting lost in fathomless bliss for sure
Let's feel each other's scars
Sooth and heal them from near or far
Come into my world of beatific smiles
And in my loving embrace see how time flies
Let silence speak the language of our hearts
Pure emotions spill, our hearts and souls merge into one, never apart !

50. I Can Feel You

I can feel you in my breath
In every thought wave on our love's ocean, in its depth
In life's every rhyme and rhythm, chime and jingle
Your thoughts and emotions, with mine intermingle
In the calm, stillness of the dawn and night
When our dreams and desires take flight
In chaos and amidst the madding crowd
Your presence with me steers through storms on a magical cloud
A panacea to my hurts, disappointment and pain
You shower with a plethora of hope, strength and good cheer rain
In the molten moon's amorous silken streams
In glistening dewdrops, and ravishing fiery dreams
I feel you in your sublime love so sanguine
In your words, gestures, actions so genuine
Souls entwined, our meeting a stroke of serendipity
Your being in my life, part of me, fills it with felicity!

Printed by Libri Plureos GmbH in Hamburg,
Germany